Your Verdict on the Empty Tomb

Val Grieve

EP

EP Books (Evangelical Press), Registered Office: 140 Coniscliffe Road, Darlington, Co Durham DL3 7RT
admin@epbooks.org
www.epbooks.org

JPL Books, 3883 Linden Ave. S.E., Wyoming, MI 49548
order@jplbooks.com
www.jplbooks.com

First published 1988

This edition 2017

British Library Cataloguing in Publication Data available

Print ISBN 978-1-78397-189-3

Contents

1 Setting the Scene

'In the world today a person who is religiously inclined is usually regarded as a crank, a killjoy, unhappy and a general bore. I was once one of those people who jeered at Christianity in this way but one day a great change took place in my life; the change from self to Christ.'

I wrote those words over forty years before this book was written, shortly after I became a Christian. As I look back on my life this was certainly the most significant thing that has happened to me. More significant than graduating from university, getting married, becoming a father, becoming a solicitor, becoming a senior partner in my firm or anything else this world has offered me.

As a child I never went to Sunday school and very seldom to church. In my early teenage years I became an atheist, quite convinced that God did not exist. My first encounter with real Christianity was when I went to Oxford University to study law. I must have been fairly intelligent, but I was certainly abysmally ignorant as to what Christianity was all about.

A fellow student at my college started telling me about his faith. He was different from anyone I had ever met before. To him God was real and relevant. I can well remember having many arguments and discussions with him. As an atheist and a budding lawyer I was quite convinced that I would soon refute his arguments about

Christianity. But this was not the case. Instead, for the first time in my life, I found myself thinking about the meaning of life and the evidence for the Christian faith. As I argued furiously with my Christian friend, I had a horrible suspicion at times that, after all, he was right and Christianity was true. This made me argue against Christianity more than ever! But one Easter Sunday everything changed.

I awoke in the morning of that day with no thoughts of Christ at all in my mind. I was as full of this world as the next person. Then suddenly the thought came to me that on Easter Sunday Jesus rose from the dead. He was alive and I could come into contact with him. Something inexplicable happened to me. I suddenly knelt down and talked to Christ. Yes, to Christ. I suddenly knew he was living, that he was near me and that he wanted to enter my life. I talked to him. I said, as far as I can remember, 'Come into my life, Lord Jesus.' As I said this, he came. Yes, he himself. I knew he was mine. A marvellous joy filled my life.

I can now look back on what happened then and can say from personal experience that conversion to Christianity is real and it lasts. Over the years, I have been asked many times how the change from being an atheist to being a Christian took place. I always reply by saying that there are two reasons for my being a Christian. Firstly, I found that Christianity is true. Secondly, I have found that it works in my life. Many people are surprised when I claim that Christianity is true. Somehow they have the idea that to become a Christian is to commit intellectual suicide. It reminds me of the teenager's definition of faith as 'believing what you know isn't true'! My experience is the exact opposite of this. One of the main reasons I became a Christian is not that I stopped thinking but that I started thinking. As I argued with my Christian friend, I saw for the first time there was much evidence in favour of Christianity.

My subsequent career as a lawyer has confirmed this. Again, this may sound surprising. Lawyers are not noted for their Christian faith. In fact, the opposite is true. Many times I have been asked how I can possibly be both a Christian and a lawyer. I usually reply by saying that I wouldn't want to be a lawyer if I weren't a Christian!

Over the years my Christian faith has strengthened, guided and judged all that I have done as a lawyer. Christianity has given me a new perspective on law, justice and other legal principles. It has also given me a sense of finiteness. Lawyers are tempted to pretend to be God and to be judgmental. Many a time I have been reminded of the saying of the old Puritan when he saw someone being taken away to the gallows to be hanged — 'There go I but for the grace of God.'

Above all, law trains one to think logically. One of my main hobbies is playing chess and the thing that always fascinates me about that game is the sheer logic of working out one's moves in advance. The law has the same fascination. Not only does it train one to think but also to seek for the truth. Lawyers know when a case has been proved and are well used to assessing evidence. When I was an atheist I had an inbuilt prejudice against the Christian faith. It was through examining the evidence that I became a Christian.

This experience of examining the evidence and then being converted to Christianity is by no means unique to me. One of America's leading lawyers a few years ago was Charles Colson. At the time of the Watergate scandal he was serving as Special Counsel to President Nixon. He was at the height of his legal career and was well known as Nixon's 'hatchet man', described by *Time* magazine as 'tough, wily, nasty and tenaciously loyal to Richard Nixon'. Suddenly in the crisis of Watergate his life was changed. He first began to consider the claims of Jesus Christ when visiting a business friend. Colson was startled to find his friend talking as if Jesus were real. Up to then, as far as Colson was concerned, Jesus was just a historical figure. His friend explained that Jesus is alive today and that his Spirit is part of today's scene. Before he left, his friend gave him a copy of *Mere Christianity* by C. S. Lewis and urged him to read it for himself. A few days later the opportunity came to do this. Colson was on holiday in a cottage by the sea. He recalled in his book *Born Again*:

> I unpacked Lewis's book and placed a yellow pad at my side to jot down key points, not unlike the way I prepared to argue a major case in court... All my training insisted that analysis precedes decision, that arguments be marshalled in two neat columns, pros and cons... On the top of the pad I wrote: Is there a God? I opened *Mere Christianity* and found myself... face to face with an intellect so disciplined, so lucid, so relentlessly logical that I could only be grateful I had never faced him in a court of law. Soon I had covered two pages of yellow paper with pros to my query, 'Is there a God?' On the con side were listed the conventional doubts so prevalent in our materialistic, science-has-all-the-answers society — we can't see, hear or feel God. Or can we?... As a lawyer I was impressed by Lewis's arguments about moral law, the existence of which he demonstrates is real, and which has been perceived with astonishing consistency in all times and places... The central thesis of Lewis's book, and the essence of Christianity, is summed up in one mind-boggling sentence: Jesus Christ is God (see John 10:30). Not just part of God, or just sent by God, or just related to God. He was (and therefore, of course, is) God. The more I grappled with those words, the more they began to explode before my eyes, blowing into smithereens a lot of comfortable old notions I had floated through life with, without thinking much about them. Lewis put it so bluntly that you can't slough it off: for Christ to have talked as he talked, lived as he lived, died as he died, he was either God or a raving lunatic. There was my choice, as simple, stark, and

frightening as that, no fine shadings, no gradations, no compromises. No one had ever thrust this truth at me in such a direct and unsettling way. I'd been content to think of Christ as an inspired prophet and teacher who walked the sands of the Holy Land 2,000 years ago — several cuts above other men of his time or, for that matter, any time. But if one thinks of Christ as no more than that, I reasoned, then Christianity is a simple palliative, like taking a sugar-coated placebo once a week on Sunday morning. On this sunny morning on the Maine coast with fresh breezes picking up off the ocean, it was hard for me to grasp the enormity of this point—that Christ is the living God who promises us a day-to-day living relationship with him and a personal one at that... And so early that Friday morning, while I sat alone staring at the sea I love, words I had not been certain I could understand or say fell naturally from my lips: 'Lord Jesus, I believe you. I accept you. Please come into my life. I commit it to you.'

In this simple way Colson's whole life was changed. Ahead of him lay seven months in prison because of his involvement in Watergate. Afterwards, he abandoned his law career and is now giving all his time to the ministry of Prison Fellowship, working amongst prisoners in many countries.

Charles Colson certainly had to do some thinking before his encounter with Jesus Christ. My aim in writing this book is to start you thinking. Before I became a Christian I was ignorant about the Christian faith. Like so many people today, I was quite sure that the Gospels were full of contradictions, but I had never even read them! It always amazes me how many people are still in that position. They are extremely knowledgeable about life, politics and every other subject under the sun. But they have never really examined the claims and teachings of Jesus. Sir Norman Anderson in his book *A Lawyer among the Theologians* has pointed out:

> Lawyers are predisposed by their training to accept the propositions that documentary evidence should, as far as possible, be allowed to speak for itself; that an honest attempt should be made to sift and assess oral testimony and not to jump to any premature conclusions that it is mutually contradictory; and that circumstantial evidence may, on occasion, be exceedingly persuasive. A lawyer, and especially a judge, is always face to face with the problem of how to evaluate evidence and distinguish the reliable from the misleading.

Ever since I became a Christian I have carefully examined the evidence for the resurrection, the physical return from the dead of Jesus Christ. My purpose in writing this book is to present this evidence to you. I claim that logic must point in the direction of his resurrection on an actual day and date in our history when, if you had been there, you could have touched the living Jesus and heard him speak. There is another reason why I have written this book. For far too long the Christian faith has been under attack. Of course, it does not really need a lawyer to defend it. As a famous preacher said many years ago, 'Defend the Bible? I would as soon defend a lion!' But, despite this, I feel it is high time someone spoke up for the Christian faith. I maintain that not only does it stand up to examination, but it is the most relevant thing in the world today.

2 The Most Important Question in the World

'If you could meet any person of the past and ask just one question, whom would you meet and what question would you ask?' When asked this, Professor Joad, then professor of philosophy at London University and not a Christian, answered, 'I would meet Jesus Christ and ask him the most important question in all the world — "Did you or did you not rise from the dead?"' Professor Joad was right. The most important question in the world is whether Jesus Christ rose from the dead and is alive today. In other words, did Easter really happen?

To start with, the resurrection is the very heart of the Christian faith. In connection with a television programme called *Credo*, a book was published entitled *In Search of Christianity*. Amongst the contributors was Colin Buchanan, the Bishop of Aston, who stated 'The Jesus Christ to whom Christians respond is not the dead (though appealing) person of the past, but the Living Lord of the present. He is the same Jesus Christ who is presented to us in the Gospels.' Any search for Christianity must begin here. Personally, the importance of the resurrection really came home to me when I was asked to speak to a university group on 'The Message of the Early Church'. In order to find out what it was, I read carefully through all the thirteen messages or sermons in the book of Acts — seven by Paul, five by Peter and one by Stephen. As I read them, I was impressed by the fact that, as recorded by Luke, they were brief and simple. Also I realised that every one of them had one thing in common, namely, Jesus is alive and he can change your life.

Peter sums it up in his message on the day of Pentecost: *This Jesus God raised up, and of that we all are witnesses* (Acts 2:32). Every sermon was an Easter sermon. The resurrection is mentioned more than one hundred times in the New Testament and nearly every book refers to it. This is what Christianity is all about: that Jesus Christ not only lived and died but on the third day he rose again from the dead. Without the resurrection there is no gospel. As Paul says, *If Christ has not been raised, your faith is futile* (1 Corinthians 15:17).

Any consideration of what Christianity is about must begin here. Yet, amazingly enough, in these days when Jesus is often in the news, this is something we have forgotten. The rock opera *Jesus Christ Superstar* ended with Jesus in the grave. Incredibly it missed out the most vital thing about the life of Christ. His death was not the end. He rose from the dead. As a former Archbishop of Canterbury, Dr Michael Ramsey, has said, 'For the first disciples, the gospel without the resurrection was not merely a gospel without its final chapter; it was not a gospel at all.'

The resurrection also makes Christianity unique. In the global village in which we live people are increasingly asking, 'What is the difference between Christianity and other religions?' The answer is basically very simple. Christianity is the only religion in the world based on the resurrection from the dead of its founder.

No Buddhist has ever claimed that Buddha rose from the dead. When he died it was a passing away in which nothing whatever remained behind. The same applied to Mohammed. According to tradition he died on the 8 June 632AD at the age of 61 in Medina, where his tomb is annually visited by thousands of devout Muslims. But down the ages the claim of Christianity is that Jesus not only died but rose from the dead and is alive today, changing people's lives. If this is true, then Christianity stands by itself. There is no real comparison with other religions because their founders are dead. Christians claim that the founder of their faith is still alive.

Many years ago a fellow lawyer, Frank Morison, started to write a book disproving the historical resurrection of Christ. He felt that the evidence for it rested upon insecure foundations. A remarkable thing happened as he was doing research for his book. As he studied the life of Christ, sifted the evidence at first hand and formed his own judgment, a revolution took place in his thinking. Instead of writing a book disproving the resurrection, the overwhelming evidence in favour of it compelled him to write a book proving it! Its first chapter was entitled 'The Book that Refused To Be Written', and his book *Who Moved the Stone?* was a bestseller for very many years.

In his play *The Vigil*, Ladislas Fodor cleverly constructs a court scene in which the evidence for the resurrection is examined. A gardener is accused of stealing Christ's body, witnesses are called and evidence is brought in court for and against him. The audience is the jury. They are drawn into the play by being asked to give a verdict at the end of it.

In the same way I want you to imagine that you are a member of the jury while I, the lawyer, present to you the evidence for Christ's resurrection.

3 The Courts and the Jury

It may be helpful first to describe how a court works. Perhaps you have never been to court. If this is so, I would certainly recommend going to see one in action. All sorts of disputes come before English courts. In fact, there are different courts for different types of cases. One basic starting point is to decide whether any case is criminal or civil. Usually this is pretty obvious. In a criminal case someone is being prosecuted for a criminal offence and in a civil case someone is being sued, say, for money he or she owes.

But whatever their differences, all court cases have one common factor. There are two parties with conflicting interests. The way of resolving their dispute is for it to be adjudicated upon by an independent person. In a serious criminal case such as murder or manslaughter this is, of course, a judge. As two parties are involved, each of them will have their own lawyer to represent their case. Each of these lawyers will call witnesses to present evidence in favour of their client. In criminal cases in the Crown Court there will also be a jury. The case must be decided by the law of the land.

Lord Denning sums it up well in a judgment of his: 'To every subject in this land, no matter how powerful, I would use Thomas Fuller's words over 300 years ago: "Be you never so high, the law is above you".' The task of the judge, besides giving sentence at the end of the case, is to see that the law is observed. It is interesting to find that the red robe which judges still wear was originally a cassock, rooting English law with the Christian faith, stressing that the law was above self and national interest. One basic principle of English law is that a person charged with committing a crime may only be tried by his equals. Generally speaking, therefore, everyone who appears before an English criminal court will have the question of guilt or innocence determined by lay men or women. If tried in a Magistrates Court it is usually determined by lay magistrates. If tried in the Crown Court it is determined by a jury. A jury consists of twelve people aged between 18 and 65 who have been resident in this country for five years. Over 200 years ago Sir William Blackstone, the great English lawyer, said in his Oxford lectures on law: 'Trial by jury ever has been, and I trust ever will be, looked upon as the glory of the English Law. It is the most transcendent privilege which any subject can enjoy, or wish for, that he cannot be affected either in his property, his liberty or his person, but by the consent of twelve of his neighbours and equals.'

I hope that I have helped to set the scene before presenting to you the evidence for the resurrection. Like the audience in the play *The Vigil* I want you to imagine that you are on a jury faced with the responsibility of giving a verdict at the end of the case.

But before I deal with your duties it is necessary to mention what lawyers call the 'standard of proof'. Suppose you are involved in a car accident and someone is injured. You are then sued in court for damages and the court has to decide whether or not you have been negligent. How does it do this? What would constitute proof?

The leading legal text book on evidence states: 'The standard of proof required in civil cases is generally expressed as proof on the balance of probabilities. If the evidence is such that the tribunal can say "We think it more probable than not", the burden is discharged, but if the probabilities are equal it is not.' When considering the evidence for the resurrection, we must apply the same 'standard of proof'. In other words, what is the most likely thing that happened?

The jury

With this in mind, let me go over the duties of a jury. One of these is that it must be unbiased. We must not be like the foreman of a jury who, when asked to give its verdict, said 'Seven of us find the prisoner guilty as charged; three of us find him as guilty as they come; and two of us find him guilty from the word "Go"!'

But to be unbiased is very often more difficult than it appears, as all of us have inbuilt prejudices. A striking example of this is the Frenchman Ernest Renan, who wrote a book, *The Life of Jesus*, in which he denounced the resurrection of Christ. Yet, by his own admission, Renan started with the presupposition: 'There is no such thing as a miracle. Therefore, the resurrection did not take place!' Such an attitude would not be tolerated in a court of law. We must be as unbiased as we can when examining the evidence. Above all, the duty of a jury is to give a verdict. In fact, the one thing that a judge never does in a criminal case is to judge. The judge presides over the court, sums up at the end of the hearing and pronounces the sentence. However, it is the jury that has to decide whether the accused is guilty or innocent, and it has a responsibility to bring in a verdict.

The evidence for the resurrection also demands a verdict. We must examine it and make up our minds as to whether or not Jesus Christ rose from the dead.

4 The Meaning of the Resurrection

What does the Bible mean when it mentions the resurrection of Jesus? What actually happened on the first Easter Sunday morning?

Resurrection is not the immortality of the soul. This was the view of Greek philosophy. The body is the prison of the soul and when it dies, the soul is released from its bondage to go to heaven. This view is reflected in the well-known words of the dying Socrates when he said, 'Catch me if you can.' Also, in the popular song about John Brown whose 'body lies a-mould'ring in the grave, but his soul goes marching on'.

Is the resurrection, then, reincarnation? This idea is found in many Eastern religions such as Hinduism and Buddhism. In Hinduism the same soul may be in one life a god, in another a human, in a third an animal or even a plant. Everything depends upon how one lived in the previous life. Any evil in this life is a punishment for the soul's behaviour in the past. This process of birth and rebirth must go on unceasingly until the ultimate state of 'nirvana' or nothingness is reached. One is then beyond feeling either pain or pleasure.

But this is not the Christian view of our future. The Bible clearly teaches *it is appointed for man to die once, and after that comes judgment* (Hebrews 9:27). Above all, resurrection means eternal life and not eternal extinction.

Is the resurrection the mere bringing back of a corpse to life? The New Testament records six instances of this. The son of the widow of Nain, Jairus's daughter, Lazarus, the saints raised at the time of the death of Jesus, Dorcas and Eutychus. But in all these cases the return to life was only temporary. Each one of these people had to die a second time. This does not apply to Jesus: *We know that Christ, being raised from the dead, will never die again; death no longer has dominion over him* (Romans 6:9).

So, the resurrection of Jesus adds a new dimension to these views. As Professor F. F. Bruce has pointed out in his 1968 book *Christianity Today*, 'To the disciples themselves, and to all other Jews of that time, resurrection meant bodily resurrection.' This is different from a mere resuscitation. Jesus, after his resurrection, was not a revived corpse. Paul states that he had a 'spiritual body' (1 Corinthians 15:44). This is a body no longer subject to the laws of nature. Jesus could suddenly appear to the disciples and then just as suddenly disappear. But Jesus was not a disembodied spirit. Not only did he expressly deny this, but he drew attention to the scars of the crucifixion. These would assure the disciples of his identity, and to handle his body would convince them of his reality (Luke 24:39). A wonderful change had taken place. Jesus was the same person and yet in other ways not the same.

The resurrection was certainly not just in the minds of the disciples. As James Dunn has said, 'By resurrection they clearly meant that something had happened to Jesus himself. God had raised him, not merely reassured them. He was alive again, made alive again with the life which is the climax of God's purpose for humankind, not merely retrieved from the jaws of death but conqueror over death, "exalted to God's right hand". It was this glowing conviction which lay at the heart of the chain reaction which began Christianity.'

5 The Historical Facts

How does a lawyer begin a legal case? Contrary to popular opinion, he or she does not begin by considering how much they intend to charge! They start with the facts. Any consideration about the resurrection of Jesus Christ must begin here.

Some years ago I took part in a mock court of inquiry into the resurrection of Jesus Christ at the College of Law at Chester. This was arranged by the Christian Union at the college, who challenged the Humanist Students' Group to hold this inquiry. At it there were counsel both for and against the resurrection. Also, expert witnesses were called. Before the inquiry, I was interested as to what line the other side would take and was somewhat surprised to find it maintaining that the whole of Christianity is a myth. Jesus Christ never existed! I had been asked to appear at the court of inquiry to give evidence for the facts about Jesus Christ. This meant that my evidence was crucial.

In my proof of evidence I stated that history tells us three facts about Jesus Christ, namely:

1.   He is a historical figure who lived nearly two thousand years ago.
2.   He was crucified on a cross and died.

3. After his body had been buried his tomb was found to be empty three days later. From that moment onwards the early Christians claimed that Jesus had risen from the dead.

These facts can be proved in three ways.

Jewish writers

The most important of these is Josephus, who was born in Jerusalem about AD37 into a distinguished Jewish family. He was well educated as a young man and, after studying the various schools of Jewish thought, became a Pharisee.

In AD64, the year of the burning of Rome, he visited that city as a member of a Jewish embassy. Clearly he was impressed by what he saw, and became friendly with members of the Emperor's family. When he returned to Jerusalem he found his own country ready to revolt against the Romans. Josephus appears to have advised against this, but was loyal to the Jewish nation. In its rebellion against Rome he became commander of the Jewish forces in Galilee.

After their defeat, he surrendered to the victorious Roman general Vespasian. He then prophesied that one day Vespasian would become emperor. Vespasian was impressed by this and kept Josephus as his prisoner. When this prediction came true in AD69 he was freed. He then joined the Roman general Titus in his siege of Jerusalem and was there when it fell in the summer of AD70.

After this, Josephus went to live in Rome where he became a close friend of the Emperor and a Roman citizen. He devoted the second half of his life to writing numerous books on the history of the Jews. One of these was a twenty-volume history of the Jewish nation covering the period from its earliest origins down to his own day and the revolt against Rome.

Josephus refers to many figures of the New Testament — Pilate, Annas, the Herods, John the Baptist and (twice) to Jesus Christ. The first reference is very brief and is about James, 'the brother of Jesus, who was called Christ'. The second reference is longer, and far more important, but it has been questioned. This is because in this text, Josephus says not too little but too much. He states that Jesus was the Messiah and that he appeared to the disciples alive again on the third day. It is argued that, as a Jew, Josephus would not have believed this and that some early Christians must have tampered with the original text. But, despite this, the text as it stands is supported with only slight variations by all the manuscripts which we have.

This question as to the original wording may be resolved by an Arabic manuscript released in 1972 by Professor Schlomo Pines of the Hebrew University in Jerusalem. This manuscript omits the disputed portions and reads:

> At this time there was a wise man who was called Jesus. And his conduct was good and [he] was known to be virtuous. And many people from among the Jews and other nations became his disciples. Pilate condemned him to be crucified and to die. And those who had become his disciples did not abandon his discipleship. They reported that he had appeared to them three days after his crucifixion and that he was alive; accordingly, he was perhaps the Messiah concerning whom the prophets have recounted wonders.

To summarise, these two passages in Josephus tell us the following facts about Jesus:

1. The time when he lived.

2. He was the brother of James.

3. He was called the Messiah by some.

4. He was known as a wise and good man.

5. He had many disciples, both Jews and Gentiles.

6. Pilate condemned him to death by crucifixion.

7. The disciples reported that Jesus had risen from the dead and that he had appeared to them on the third day after his crucifixion.

8. As a result the disciples continued to proclaim his teachings.

There are other references to Jesus in Jewish literature, the most important of which is that preserved in the tract Sanhedrin. This confirms that Jesus was hanged on Passover Eve and that this was an offence against Jewish religious laws.

Pagan writers

It is interesting to find that the first mention in Roman literature of Christ and the Christians is in the police news of that day. According to the Romans, Caesar was Lord, but according to the early Christians Jesus was Lord. This inevitably brought them into conflict with Rome and its Emperor.

Cornelius Tacitus (AD55-120) was a Roman historian who lived through the reigns of over half-a-dozen Roman emperors. He was son-in-law of Julius Agricula, Governor of Britain from AD80 to 84. He has been called 'The Greatest Historian of Ancient Rome' and is generally acknowledged amongst scholars for his moral integrity and essential goodness.

One of his works is the *Annals* covering the history of Rome from the death of Augustus in AD14 to that of Nero in AD68. In this he mentions the famous fire of Rome in AD64 and Nero's attempt to blame the Christians for this instead of himself:

> To kill the rumours, Nero charged and tortured some people hated for their evil practices — the group popularly known as 'Christians'. The founder of this sect, Christ, had been put to death by the governor of Judea, Pontius Pilate, when Tiberius was Emperor. Their deadly superstition had been suppressed

temporarily, but was beginning to spring up again — not now just in Judea but even in Rome itself where all kinds of sordid and shameful activities are attracted and catch on.

First those who confessed to being Christians were arrested. Then, on information obtained from them, hundreds were convicted, more for their anti-social beliefs than for fire raising. In their deaths they were made a mockery. They were covered in the skins of wild animals, torn to death by dogs, crucified or set on fire — so that when darkness fell they burned like torches in the night. Nero opened up his own gardens for this spectacle and gave a show in the arena where he mixed with the crowd, or stood dressed as a charioteer on a chariot. As a result, although they were guilty of being Christians and deserved death, people began to feel sorry for them. For they realized that they were being massacred not for the public good but to satisfy one man's mania.

This account shows how fair Tacitus was as a pagan to the early Christians. It has been pointed out that his evidence is not as direct as that of Josephus. He only records what was believed about Christ at that time. Notwithstanding this, his account is important. There was hardly enough time between that of Christ and his account for any legend to have developed. His account must, therefore, have a factual basis. It has even been suggested that Tacitus may have obtained his information from one of Pilate's reports to the Emperor, to which he would probably have had access because of his standing with the government.

Tacitus, then, gives us the following information:

1. Christians were named after their founder, Christ.

2. Christ was put to death by Pontius Pilate.

3. This was during the reign of the Emperor Tiberius (AD14-37).

4. His death ended the 'superstition' for a short time, but it soon broke out again.

5. It was especially popular in Judea where it began.

6. It then spread to Rome.

7. When the Great Fire of Rome destroyed a large part of the city, Nero blamed the Christians.

8. They were arrested and persecuted for their faith.

9. This was recognised as being unjust, and many Romans felt sorry for the early Christians.

10. It was recognised that they were being punished not for the public good but to satisfy the mania of Nero.

Shortly after this, Pliny the Younger gives a full and interesting account of Christianity in a letter written to the Emperor Trajan in AD112. He had a habit of writing to the Emperor on every occasion and has been described as one of the world's great letter writers. For example, from him we learn about the terrible eruption of Vesuvius in AD79. Pliny was a typical civil servant always asking for instructions. During his time as administrator of the Roman province of Bithynia in north-west Asia Minor, Christian influence was so strong that the pagan temples had become deserted. Pliny was unsure of how to deal with the Christians and wrote to the Emperor for instructions. In his letter we find an account of the early Christian worship of Christ:

> They [the Christians] were in the habit of meeting on a certain fixed day before it was light, when they sang in alternate verses a hymn to Christ, as to a god, and bound themselves by a solemn oath, not to any wicked deeds, but never to commit any fraud, theft or adultery, never to falsify their word, nor deny a trust when they should be called upon to deliver it up: After which it was their custom to separate, and then re-

assemble to partake of food — but food of an ordinary and innocent kind.

From this letter we learn several more facts about Jesus and early Christianity:

1. The early Christians met regularly (probably on a Sunday).

2. They sang hymns.

3. They worshipped Christ as God.

4. They pledged themselves not to do anything wicked.

5. They lived exemplary moral lives.

6. There is a probable reference to the Lord's Supper in the remark about their re-assembling to eat food of an ordinary kind.

The New Testament

Sometimes opponents of the Christian faith try to rule out the evidence of the Gospel writers, but this cannot be done. Their accounts are either those of eyewitnesses or based on the testimony of those who were eyewitnesses. It is illogical to dismiss them by saying that they were Christians. Their evidence should be accepted along with that of anyone else. Otherwise it is like a judge in a murder case refusing to admit the evidence of anyone who has seen the murder!

When assessing the reliability of ancient historical documents, four points should be noted:

1. The date of the original writings.

2. The date of the earliest copy available.

3. The time span between the original writing and the earliest copy.

4. The number of copies available.

When these tests are applied to the evidence of the Gospel writers, we find their reliability outstanding.

1. Jesus was crucified in the early 30s and the earliest Gospel was probably written by the 60s. This gives a time gap between Jesus and the first Gospel of about 25 years. Contrary to what is sometimes said, events in the Gospels are clearly within living memory.

2. Near my office in Manchester there is in the John Rylands Library a fragment of John's Gospel dated around AD130. It is by half a century the earliest fragment of the New Testament.

3. The time between this fragment and the original is about 40 years. (By way of contrast, the time between the original of Caesar's *Gallic War* and the earliest copy is 900 years.) Also, we have the Bodmer Papyrus containing most of John's Gospel with a time span of about 70 years and the Chester Beatty Papyri containing most of the New Testament giving a time span of about 110 years.

4. There is the staggering number of over 13,000 ancient Greek manuscripts of the New Testament in whole or in part and the text is the same in over 98 per cent of these. Again, by way of contrast, there are only nine different copies of Caesar's *Gallic War*.

No wonder Sir Frederick Kenyon (one of the greatest New Testament authorities of the past) said, 'It cannot be too strongly asserted that in substance the text of the Bible is certain. Especially is this the case with the New Testament. The number of manuscripts of the New Testament, of early translations from it, and of quotations from it in the oldest writers of the Church, is so large that it is practically certain that the true reading of every doubtful passage is preserved in some one or other of these ancient authorities. This can be said of no other ancient book in the world.'

Lawyers are used to assessing the reliability of evidence. One basic rule is that where ancient documents are involved they should be allowed to speak for themselves. In his book *A Lawyer among the Theologians* Sir Norman Anderson QC has pointed out: 'The account should be accepted as prima facie reliable unless there is evidence to show that the opposite is the case' (p.25).

6 The Empty Tomb

These facts about Jesus that we have looked at are what lawyers call common ground. Now they have been established it is necessary to consider their implication. When dealing with a legal case very often there is one fact which is the key factor. In this case it is the empty tomb of Jesus. By itself it does not prove the resurrection, but some explanation for it must be found.

Before considering various explanations, it is necessary to establish that the tomb was in fact empty. Sometimes it is said that because Paul does not mention it in his New Testament writings he did not believe that it was empty. This is a weak argument because Paul assumes that his readers knew the facts about Jesus which were in living memory. For instance, he does not mention the Sermon on the Mount, but no one has suggested that it was never preached! Also, Paul's silence about the empty tomb is more apparent than real. In 1 Corinthians 15 he states that Jesus 'was buried' and 'he was raised on the third day', clearly implying a bodily resurrection from the dead and consequently an empty tomb.

Apart from this, we find all four Gospel writers describing in detail how the tomb was found to be empty. First we see the women, who had carefully watched from a distance the burial of Jesus, coming back to the tomb early on the Sunday morning and finding to their utter astonishment that the stone was rolled away and the body was gone.

Then we discover them running back to Jerusalem and reporting this to the apostles. Peter and John rushed to the tomb and found that what the women said was true. The tomb was indeed empty. Then, the guards who were appointed to watch the tomb came into the city and reported to the Chief Priests that it was empty.

Finally, the Sanhedrin itself bears witness to the fact that the tomb was empty. They concocted a story which they commanded the soldiers to repeat thereafter to explain how the tomb became empty, namely, that the body was stolen by the disciples. We thus find a fourfold testimony to the fact of the empty tomb. In those days the Jewish people venerated the burial places of prophets and martyrs. However, it is highly significant that there is no evidence whatsoever for the tomb of Jesus being honoured in this way. The only explanation is that it was empty and there was no body to venerate. If this were not the case, all that the Romans and Jews had to do to refute Christianity was to produce the dead body of Jesus. They were clearly not able to do this. So, the point at issue was not whether the tomb was empty but how it became empty.

A Jewish scholar, Geza Vermes, sums it up well: 'In the end, when every argument has been considered and weighed, the only conclusion acceptable to the historian must be... that the women who set out to pay their last respects to Jesus found to their consternation, not a body, but an empty tomb.'

This leads us to the vital question: 'What happened to Jesus?' How did his tomb become empty? It is a question that cannot be avoided, and a verdict must be reached.

Some years ago a leading American biblical scholar, Dr Wilbur M. Smith, wrote to twenty fellow scholars asking them how they accounted for the tomb being found empty. Amazingly, one of them replied that he could no more explain how the tomb became empty than he could explain how Santa Claus comes down the chimney at Christmas time! Sadly, that New Testament scholar had missed the whole point of the resurrection. We are not dealing with a myth, but with the greatest question we can ever consider together. Did Jesus really rise from the dead? How did his tomb become empty? We must give a verdict and there are four possible explanations as to what happened. Each of these can be summed up in one word — fraud, swoon, hallucination and miracle. We must now examine each of these and decide which of them is the most likely.

Fraud

In Matthew's Gospel we find the earliest explanation of how the tomb of Jesus became empty. After he was crucified, the Jewish authorities asked permission of Pontius Pilate for a guard to be mounted outside the tomb in case his body was stolen. Pilate gave his permission for this and a guard then made the tomb secure and stood outside watching over it. Amongst scholars there has been some discussion as to whether this was a Jewish or Roman guard. In many ways this does not matter, because in both cases the guard was formidable.

In the case of a Jewish guard, if a guard member fell asleep he was beaten and burned with his own clothes. A member of such a guard was also forbidden to sit down or to lean against anything when on duty. However, I am inclined to agree with those scholars who opt for a Roman guard and I will assume that this was the case.

Matthew records the official Jewish explanation as to what happened after the guard had taken up its place and was on duty. This must have been the current belief among many Jewish people at that time or he would not have thought of exposing it. According to this explanation, the guard fell asleep and the disciples came by night and stole the body of Jesus. They then invented the story that he had risen from the dead and perpetrated what must be the biggest and longest-lasting hoax of all time.

Let me summarise some of the arguments which show that this explanation is, to say the least, far-fetched:

1. If this is what really happened, why were the early disciples not charged with stealing the body of Jesus? According to Roman law the body of a condemned criminal belonged to the state. This was why Joseph had to ask the permission of Pilate to bury the body of Jesus. To steal a body was a serious offence and it is certainly strange that both the Roman and Jewish authorities did nothing to substantiate this charge against the disciples.

2. The disciples were in no fit state to steal the body. Their number was down to a handful and only two men, namely Peter and John, appear to have been in Jerusalem at that time. Peter had just denied his Lord and John was busy looking after the mother of Jesus. They were depressed, afraid and leaderless. It seems inconceivable that they could have then suddenly become brave and daring enough to face the Roman guard at the tomb and steal the body of Jesus.

3. We also need to ask what motive these disciples would have had for stealing the body? As every lawyer knows, behind nearly every crime there is a motive. What was the motive here? Nearly every one of the early disciples died for his faith. Why did they do this? They had nothing to gain but everything to lose. People may die for what they sincerely believe is true, but it is another thing to die for what you know is a deliberate lie.

4. The story of the guards does not stand up to examination. From Roman history we know a great deal about the Roman army and its strict military discipline. According to a Roman military historian, the Roman guard was a sixteen man security unit, each man of which was trained to protect six square feet of ground. If one man of the guard failed in his duty, he was automatically executed along with the other fifteen. Members of such a guard were well aware of the punishment that awaited them all if just one fell asleep or left his position. In view of this, it seems incredible that the whole of the Roman guard fell asleep on duty at the same time. Further, if I had the guard commander in court for cross-examination, I would just like to ask him one question:

'If you were asleep, how do you know what happened?' Believe me, a story like this would be laughed out of court in no time.

5. In addition, if the disciples stole the body of Jesus, they certainly appear to have been singularly inept. John records in his Gospel that when he and Peter arrived at the empty tomb, they found inside it the linen clothes which had been wrapped around the body of Jesus when he was buried. If the body was stolen, what was the point in leaving the grave clothes behind? Surely, it would have been far easier to have removed the body as it was. Especially as time was at a premium with, according to this explanation, the Roman guard conveniently asleep outside! A small detail like this speaks volumes.

6. If the disciples stole the body, they would never have got away with it. Sooner or later one of them would have had to tell the truth. Charles Colson says that one of the lessons of the Watergate scandal was that a lie cannot live for long. 'With the most powerful office in the world at stake, a small band of hand picked loyalists, no more than ten of us, could not hold a conspiracy together for more than two weeks.' It would also have been impossible for the early disciples to cover up what they had done. Eventually Peter or one of the others would have split and told the truth to save his own life.

7. We have already seen that the Jews venerated the burial places of their religious leaders. If the body had been stolen, it must have been buried elsewhere. But there is no trace whatsoever of any place in the vicinity of Jerusalem being venerated as the place where Christ's body was eventually buried. Why is this so? The answer is that there was no body to venerate.

8. Fraud would also mean that the early disciples were not just deceived but deliberate deceivers, who perpetrated the greatest confidence trick of all time. Yet we find Roman historians like Tacitus and Pliny commending the early Christians for their upright and moral lives. Their known moral character and teaching is contrary to the accusation that they stole the body

and were fraudulent. As Joseph Klausner, a Jewish scholar, has said, 'Deliberate imposture is not the substance out of which the religion of millions of mankind is created... the nineteen hundred years' faith of millions is not founded on deception.'

Swoon

All of us must have read accounts of people who have been thought to be dead and have suddenly recovered. One example of this was the case that occurred in England of a 72-year-old man who apparently came back to life after suffering a heart attack. An explanation about 200 years old maintains that this is what happened in Jesus' case. Jesus did not die on the cross, but fainted or swooned from exhaustion. He was taken down from the cross and placed in the cool of the tomb, where he then revived. After this he emerged from the tomb and the disciples wrongly jumped to the conclusion that he had risen from the dead.

This explanation has come into prominence through a Muslim sect called the Ahmadiya. They maintain that after Jesus escaped from the tomb he met the disciples in Galilee and then walked on to North India; he finally died at the age of 120 and was buried in Kashmir in the tomb of an unknown sheikh. This sect is regarded by orthodox Muslims as heretical and its claim is not supported by any valid evidence.

This explanation was also given a modern twist by Dr Hugh J. Schonfield in his book *The Passover Plot*. He maintains that Jesus intended to fake his death and planned that he should then come back alive. When he cried out on the cross 'I thirst' he was drugged with wine. Unfortunately the plot failed when the Roman soldier pierced the side of Jesus with a spear. This wound was fatal. An 'unknown young man' went to tell the disciples what had happened, but he was mistaken for Jesus. The disciples then believed that Jesus had risen from the dead!

To sum up the 'swoon' explanation: we are dealing here with a case of resuscitation and not resurrection. Is this so? Did Jesus really die on the cross? Was he drugged? It is significant to find that no suggestion of this kind has come down to us from the past, despite all the violent attacks which have been made on the Christian faith. Again, there are many arguments against this theory:

1. In those days crucifixion was a common occurrence. It was originally devised by the Phoenicians and then adopted by the Romans, mainly because it was a cruel and slow way of putting someone to death. History records that on one occasion 6,000 men were crucified in one day. Roman soldiers became experts at it and reduced it to an exact science with a set of rules to be followed. They knew their job well. It was more than their lives were worth to make a mistake when dealing with Jesus, especially after the governor Pontius Pilate had personally condemned him to death.

2. In Jerusalem a skeleton of a man crucified in the first century was found. From it we know a great deal about the facts of crucifixion. As already mentioned, it was a slow way of putting someone to death. Contrary to what is commonly believed, the nails did not kill the victim but crucifixion was an asphyxial death. The victim had to push his body up in order to breath. Eventually exhaustion made this impossible and a painful death followed. One way of hastening death was to break the legs of the victim so that he could no longer push himself up. The skeleton found has bones broken in this way. This information helps to confirm the account of the crucifixion of Jesus found in the Gospels. We find there that the legs of the two thieves were broken. This was because the Passover began at sunset and according to Jewish law bodies could not be left on the cross on that day. In the case of Jesus, it was so obvious that he was dead that his legs were not broken. Again it seems incredible that the Roman soldiers should bungle something like this. Also Pilate would never have given permission for Joseph to bury the body of Jesus unless he was absolutely convinced that he was dead.

3. This explanation also ignores what to me seems a very important detail. John writes that one of the Roman soldiers pierced the side of Jesus with a spear and at once there came out blood and water (John 19:34). This is the kind of detail which only an eyewitness would notice. From a medical point of view this reference to water is particularly significant. Schonfield conveniently ignores this important detail and does not even mention it. He also maintains that the emission of blood shows that Jesus was still alive — but this is wrong as there can be bleeding after death. What then is the explanation of the blood and water? The most probable one was given by Professor Rendle Short, late Professor of Surgery at Bristol University. He states:

> As a result of the spiritual and physical agony endured, the deep distress in Gethsemane, the insults in the high priest's house, and the appalling brutality of a Roman scourging, a condition of acute dilation of the stomach may have developed, and the spear wound drew watery fluid from the stomach, and blood from the heart and great vessels of the thorax... Needless to say, such a wound would be instantly fatal if the victim was not already dead, as indeed he was.

4. Then, too, if Jesus revived in the tomb he must have been in an extremely weak condition. Before his crucifixion he endured a Roman flogging. Without going into details this was very often enough in itself to kill a man. It left him so weak that he was unable, as was customary, to carry his own cross. He was then crucified and left to hang on the cross through the mounting heat of the day. After this, he was without food or water for three days. How was it that in this extremely weak condition he was ever able to convince anyone that he was conqueror over death and the grave? In the nineteenth century the German liberal thinker David Strauss, himself a sceptic, admitted this when he said:

It is impossible that a being who had stolen half-dead out of the sepulchre, who crept about weak and ill, wanting medical treatment, who required bandaging, strengthening and indulgence, and who still at last yielded to his sufferings, could have given to the disciples the impression that he was a conqueror over death and the grave, the Prince of Life, an impression which lay at the bottom of their future ministry. Such a resuscitation could by no possibility have changed their sorrow into enthusiasm, and elevated their reverence into worship.

5. We also have to answer the question as to how Jesus escaped from the tomb. There are three things he had to escape from. First, there were his grave clothes. Within a few hours the spices would have hardened around them, making escape extremely difficult. Then, how did Jesus escape from the tomb itself? There was a large stone at its mouth, secured in place by a groove. It would be virtually impossible to move this from inside the tomb. Finally, how did he escape from the guards unless they were conveniently asleep!

6. Finally, if the 'swoon' theory is correct, Jesus must have perpetrated a deliberate fraud by passing himself off as one risen from the dead. The least he could have done was to have told his disciples that he had had a narrow escape. The previous explanation leaves us with fraudulent disciples, but this one leaves us with a fraudulent Jesus. This is contrary to his known moral character and even more difficult to believe.

Hallucination

Hallucinations often occur when someone longs for something so much that eventually they believe it has happened, like the wife who loses a loved husband. For years she has been used to him coming home from work at 6.00PM. Each evening at this time she thinks of him and longs to see him again. Eventually she believes that her husband has at long last come home and has spoken to her.

According to this third explanation of the empty tomb, this is what happened to the disciples. Since they were so confident that Jesus would rise from the dead, they eventually believed it had happened. Ernest Renan, referring to Mary Magdalene, said: 'The passion of an hallucinated woman gives to the world a resurrected God.' According to the American Psychiatric Association's official glossary, a hallucination is 'a false sensory perception in the absence of an actual external stimulus'. In popular language, the idea that Jesus rose from the dead was wish fulfilment and it was 'all in the mind'. At first sight this particular explanation seems plausible, but further consideration raises some strong objections:

1. Its basic assumption is that the disciples expected Jesus to rise from the dead. But the reverse is the case. The resurrection caught the disciples by surprise. Each time Jesus appeared to them he was both unexpected and unaccepted. They were unbelieving and incredulous. The truth is that it was not the disciples who convinced themselves that Jesus was alive — it was Jesus who had to convince them. Also, as has been pointed out by David Holloway:

> A hallucination means seeing something else, and mistaking it for what you are looking for. But in the New Testament record of the resurrection appearances you get the very opposite of that. Mary did not see the gardener near the tomb and think he was Jesus. She saw Jesus and thought he was the gardener. The two on the road to Emmaus did not see a stranger and think he was Jesus. They saw Jesus and thought he was a stranger. The apostles in the upper room did not see a ghost and think it was Jesus. They saw Jesus and thought they had seen a ghost.

2. Generally only certain kinds of people, such as the highly imaginative, suffer from hallucinations. It might be said that Mary Magdalene was in this category. But we find that the appearances of Jesus were not restricted to those of any particular psychological make-up. All types of people claimed to have seen him, including a doubting Thomas, a hard-headed tax collector, Paul the intellectual and some down-to-earth fishermen.

3. Hallucinations are very individualistic and extremely subjective. They are linked to an individual's past experience and to his sub-conscious. It is highly unlikely that two persons would have the same hallucination at the same time. But here we find not only the disciples but also a group of over 500 men who all saw Christ alive again after his resurrection (1 Corinthians 15:6).

4. Another characteristic of hallucinations is that they are usually restricted to certain times and places. They require favourable circumstances. But Jesus appeared at all times of the day in all sorts of places — early in the morning, in the afternoon, in the evening and then in the garden, in a crowded room, on top of a mountain, on the road and by the sea-shore. The circumstances could hardly have been more varied.

5. Psychiatrists tell us that hallucinations usually increase in intensity and occur regularly over a long period. They become worse and very often obsessional, resulting in insanity. But with the disciples they stopped suddenly after only forty days and did not occur again.

We can thus see that the explanation that the disciples were suffering from hallucinations is contrary to the usual pattern in cases of this nature. But, above all, any explanation as to how the tomb of Jesus became empty must cover all the facts. This one does not. If the disciples imagined that Jesus had appeared to them, then all the Jews had to do was to produce his body. However, they were not able to do this because there was no body to produce. The tomb was empty! Our original question 'What happened to Jesus?'

still stands.

Miracle

Sometimes it is said that the accounts of miracles in the Gospels are a later invention of the early Christians who believed in Jesus for other reasons. But the accounts of the miracles are an integral part of the gospel message and appear in the very earliest accounts about Jesus.

It is clear that the answer of the early Christians to the question 'What happened to Jesus?' is that a miracle took place. According to them he rose from the dead, leaving an empty tomb. He then appeared to them and changed their lives. The gospel message is *that Christ died for our sins in accordance with the Scriptures, that he was buried, that he was raised on the third day in accordance with the Scriptures* (1 Corinthians 15:3, 4).

Try to be unbiased. Most of us have a basic prejudice against supernatural explanations and dismiss a miracle as a possibility without really examining it. But if we believe that God exists, and that he made and upholds the universe, there should be no difficulty in believing that he has enough power to do miracles within his creation. Even if we only admit the possibility of God, then we must also admit the possibility of a miracle. And as no one can prove that God does not exist, the possibility of a miracle can never be entirely ruled out. Don't be like the man who once said, 'I've made up my mind — don't confuse me with the facts!'

What then are the facts? What evidence is there for the miracle of the resurrection of Christ from the dead? There is certainly much more evidence than most people think. A survey among students at a technical college revealed that a majority of those who didn't believe in the resurrection had not studied the evidence! As a lawyer, let me bring to your attention three types of evidence for the resurrection, so that before you reach a verdict you are fully aware of the facts.

7 Direct Evidence

One Easter Sunday morning I was speaking at a family church service with just about every age present from 8 to 80. I began my talk by telling the congregation that they were going to see something that they had probably never seen before. This certainly got their interest. Then, much to the amazement of all, I took a daffodil out of a vase and ate it! When the congregation had recovered (along with myself!) I asked the question, 'Suppose after this service you saw a policeman and you told him that the preacher had just eaten a daffodil. Would he believe you?' Immediately a boy put up his hand and said, 'He would have to, because there are lots of us and we saw it for ourselves.'

That boy had got the point. I was trying to show the power of an eyewitness. In fact, this sort of evidence is so strong that a famous QC once said, 'When I have a poor case in court, I make a long speech; but when I have a really strong case, I simply call the witnesses.'

He was right. In any court of law the best evidence is what lawyers call 'direct evidence'. This deals with the fact in issue, which in this case is whether or not Jesus Christ rose from the dead. The best direct evidence would be that of witnesses who actually saw him after his resurrection, and that is exactly what we have in the pages of the New Testament.

When dealing with a court case, lawyers prepare a list of witnesses together with a 'proof of evidence' obtained from each of them. Paul, writing to the church at Corinth, gives us his witness list, telling us that when Jesus rose from the dead *he appeared to*

Cephas [Peter], *then to the twelve. Then he appeared to more than five hundred brothers at one time, most of whom are still alive, though some have fallen asleep. Then he appeared to James, then to all the apostles. Last of all, as to one untimely born, he appeared also to me* (1 Corinthians 15:5-8).

Paul's list is particularly impressive bearing in mind that he wrote his first letter to the Corinthians in about AD56, and the list contained in it was probably obtained during his first visit to Jerusalem in AD34. This takes us back to within three years of the resurrection itself. The list is evidently in chronological order. Also, it appears to be an official list of witnesses as it omits the evidence of any of the women who saw Jesus. Paul knew that in those days the evidence of a woman would not have been valid in a court of law.

Added to this list we also have the evidence of the Gospels, each of which contains accounts of how Jesus rose from the dead and appeared to his disciples. From Paul's list of witnesses, and the Gospels, we find that there are no less than twelve such appearances. From these we can compile a 'proof of evidence' for each of these appearances.

Mary Magdalene

It is significant that the first human being to see Jesus was a woman. We have already noted that in those days in Jewish law a woman's witness was not readily accepted. Certainly if the story of this appearance was invented, it would start with Jesus appearing to a man — either one of the disciples, such as Peter, or even one of his enemies, such as Caiaphas, the high priest.

Mary Magdalene had accompanied Mary the mother of James, Salome and Joanna when they visited the tomb of Jesus early in the morning and found it empty. She ran back to the city and told Peter and John, *"They have taken the Lord out of the tomb and we don't know where they have put him!"* (John 20:2). Peter and John then went to investigate for themselves and found that the tomb was indeed empty. After examining it they went back home.

Apparently Mary then went back to the tomb and stood outside crying. As she did so she turned around and saw Jesus standing nearby, but she did not recognise him; she thought he was the gardener. But when Jesus spoke to her, *Woman, why are you crying? Who is it you are looking for?*, she replied, *Sir, if you have carried him away, tell me where you have put him, and I will get him* (John 20:15, 16). It was then that Jesus called her by name, 'Mary.'

Clearly Mary was not expecting to see Jesus. She had not looked at him carefully, or possibly her eyes were dimmed with tears, and it was still dark at that early morning hour. But when she heard her name, she immediately recognised his voice, and replied, '*Rabboni*,' Aramaic for 'Teacher.' Mary then rushed back to the disciples with the news, 'I have seen the Lord!'

Mary mother of James, Salome and Joanna

The second appearance was to these women. Apparently, after she saw Jesus, Mary Magdalene went to John's house to tell him, Peter and the others the good news. These women then volunteered to go and tell the remainder of the disciples who were at Bethany. On the way there, probably near the Mount of Olives, *Jesus met them and said, "Greetings!" And they came up and took hold of his feet and worshiped him* (Matthew 28:9). Again this appearance was unexpected. Also, as with Mary Magdalene, these women touched the body of Jesus.

Peter

He is the first person mentioned in Paul's list of witnesses, and is the first of the apostles to meet the risen Jesus.

It is generally agreed that Mark obtained most of the information in his Gospel from Peter. Therefore, it is significant that Mark mentions this appearance, as Peter probably told him about it first-hand. Luke also mentions it in his Gospel (Luke 24:34). But both these Gospels are completely silent as to details. This was a private appearance to reassure Peter, who had just denied his Lord. The Gospels do not give a detailed account of it. Rather than making one up, which would have been natural, they simply mention it.

Two disciples on the road to Emmaus

This appearance took place on the afternoon of the first Easter Day. One of the disciples was Cleopas; perhaps the other was his wife. The two of them were walking along the road from Jerusalem to Emmaus, about seven miles away. Earlier that day they had received the report from the women that the tomb of Jesus was empty (Luke 24:9). They were discussing this together and trying to find some satisfactory explanation when Jesus came up and walked along beside them.

He asked what they were discussing so earnestly and why they were so sad. Cleopas replied, *"Are you the only visitor to Jerusalem who does not know the things that have happened there in these days?"* Cleopas then told this 'stranger' about Jesus, his crucifixion, the empty tomb and the report of his resurrection. He responded by explaining to them how these events had been foretold in the Old Testament Scriptures, but they still did not recognise him.

When they arrived at their destination the two disciples turned to Jesus and said, *"Stay with us, for it is toward evening and the day is now far spent." So he went in to stay with them. When he was at table with them, he took the bread and blessed and broke it and gave it to them. And their eyes were opened, and they recognized him. And he vanished from their sight* (Luke 24:29-31).

Again, we find these two disciples failed initially to recognise Jesus. This may seem strange, especially as they had walked and talked with him for nearly two hours. The explanation must be that they were bewildered, perplexed and anxious to get home after their visit to Jerusalem. All their hopes were ended. Jesus was dead and any thought of his resurrection was beyond their comprehension.

To the disciples, Thomas being absent

This is the last of the five appearances of Jesus that day. It took place in the evening, probably in the upper room in which Jesus had instituted the Lord's Supper. It is recorded in both Luke and John's Gospels, giving us two independent accounts as to what happened.

By now the eleven disciples (Judas Iscariot having hung himself), who had been scattered, were meeting along with others behind locked doors because of their fear of the Jewish authorities. As they discussed the report about Jesus being alive and appearing to Peter, the two from Emmaus arrived and told how they had met Jesus. *As they were talking about these things, Jesus himself stood among them, and said to them, "Peace to you!" But they were startled and frightened and thought they saw a spirit. And he said to them, "Why are you troubled, and why do doubts arise in your hearts? See my hands and my feet, that it is I myself. Touch me, and see. For a spirit does not have flesh and bones as you see that I have"* (Luke 24:36- 39). Jesus invited them to touch his hands and feet so that they could be sure that he was alive. He then sat down and ate a piece of broiled fish in their presence. Both Luke and John stress in their accounts that Jesus appeared physically. He could be touched, had flesh and bones, and sat down and ate with them. This was no ghost or spirit. Jesus had a real body.

To the disciples, Thomas being present

This appearance took place just one week after the last one. The disciples were once again gathered in the upper room, but this time Thomas was with them.

Sometimes it is said that Jesus only appeared to those who were expecting him to do so. This was certainly not the case with Thomas. The claim by the other disciples that they had seen Jesus was met with incredulity. Thomas demanded proof. *"Unless I see in his hands the mark of the nails, and place my finger into the mark of the nails, and place my hand into his side, I will never believe"* (John 20:25). Thomas wanted to see for himself. No one could have been more sceptical than he was.

Then, in the same way as before, Jesus suddenly appeared. He met the conditions of Thomas. *"Put your finger here, and see my hands; and put out your hand, and place it in my side. Do not disbelieve, but believe"* (John 20:27). At the sight of Jesus all Thomas's doubts disappeared. Not only did he see and believe, but he was the first person to acknowledge Jesus as God. He saw what the resurrection meant. Mere men do not rise from the dead. Jesus is God.

To seven disciples in Galilee

The account of this appearance ends John's Gospel. The disciples were Simon Peter, Thomas, Nathanael, the sons of Zebedee and two others (John 21:2). This is the third time that Jesus appeared to a group of his disciples. They had now left Jerusalem and returned to their home country, Galilee. They were all fishermen and Peter, who was once again the leader, proposed a fishing trip. But after a night of fishing they had caught nothing.

Towards daybreak a stranger on the sea-shore asked whether they had caught anything. When they answered 'No', he told them to cast a net on the right side of the boat. They did this and caught so many fish that they could not pull in the net. Suddenly John recognised who the stranger was. He cried out, 'It is the Lord.'

Peter, in his usual impetuous way, jumped into the water, dragging the net full of fish with him, and made his way to the shore. There the disciples found that Jesus had already anticipated their arrival. A charcoal fire was burning with fish on it and some bread. Jesus invited the disciples to come and have breakfast, and they ate with him.

Again we find that the appearance was sudden and unexpected. Jesus appeared in new surroundings in Galilee. In a leisurely way the disciples ate with him around the fire. They had plenty of time to realise that it really was Jesus who was with them. This was no hallucination.

To eleven disciples

This appearance was on a hill in Galilee where Jesus had told them to go. Very little is recorded about the details. But during it Jesus gave these disciples his great missionary commission, "*Go therefore and make disciples of all nations*" (Matthew 28:19). Though some still doubted, this was the first time that the disciples worshipped Jesus. Slowly they were realising that he was God.

To five hundred men

The following is mentioned by Paul in his list of witnesses: *Then he appeared to more than five hundred brothers at one time, most of whom are still alive, though some have fallen asleep.* (1 Corinthians 15:6). No details are given about this appearance of Jesus. Probably it was about three or four weeks after his resurrection and was in the open air on a hillside in Galilee. Nearly all of the five hundred must have been young men because thirty years later, when writing to the Corinthians, Paul states that most of them are still alive. Obviously, Paul had met many of those who were present on this occasion. As Professor Sir Norman Anderson has pointed out:

> This is one of the most significant statements in the whole of the New Testament. Paul was no fool, and he knew perfectly well that he had a host of enemies eager to pounce on him if he made any questionable statement. So it is exceedingly unlikely that he would have staked his whole credibility on the fact that there were three or four hundred persons still alive who claimed to have seen the risen Christ if this had not

been the simple truth. It was tantamount to saying, "If you don't believe me, there are plenty of people who can confirm this statement. Go and ask them."

To James

This appearance is mentioned by Paul in his list of witnesses. Paul must have heard about it from James himself during his visit to Jerusalem three years after his own conversion (Galatians 1:18, 19). James was the brother of Jesus and the Gospels record that he, along with his other younger brothers, did not believe in Jesus during his lifetime.

They accused him of ambition, self-seeking, hypocrisy and even being out of his mind. John's Gospel tells us that after the crucifixion of Jesus, his mother was not committed to their care, but to his. Six weeks later, at the time of the Ascension, we find these brothers meeting for prayer along with the other disciples. They had become believers, and not only James but all of them had seen their brother Jesus after he rose from the dead.

To eleven disciples on the Mount of Olives

Referring to Jesus and the apostles, Luke tells us that *He presented himself alive to them after his suffering by many proofs, appearing to them during forty days and speaking about the kingdom of God* (Acts 1:3).

We do not know whether there were any other appearances than those we have listed, but the last recorded appearance was on the Mount of Olives. As these apostles watched, Jesus *was lifted up, and a cloud took him out of their sight* (Acts 1:9). Once again this was a bodily appearance. How could one watch anyone ascend to heaven unless they could be seen?

To Paul

At the end of his list of witnesses in 1 Corinthians 15 Paul includes himself; *last of all, as to one untimely born, he appeared also to me* (v. 8). Paul regarded this appearance as exceptional because it took place after the ascension of Jesus into heaven. We find it described in detail three times in the Acts of the Apostles, showing how important it was (Acts 9:3-6; 22:6-10; 26:12-18).

Before his conversion Paul (then named Saul) was Public Enemy No. 1 of the early church. In his zeal he persecuted the early Christians and even obtained a warrant from the High Priest to go to Damascus and arrest any Christians he found there. But on his way to Damascus, something happened to Paul that completely changed his life: *... suddenly a light from heaven shone around him. And falling to the ground he heard a voice saying to him, "Saul, Saul, why are you persecuting me?" And he said, "Who are you, Lord?" And he said, "I am Jesus, whom you are persecuting. But rise and enter the city, and you will be told what you are to do"* (Acts 9:3-6).

In that dramatic moment Paul suddenly and unexpectedly became a Christian. His companions had heard a sound and saw the light, but Paul actually heard the voice of Jesus and saw him for himself. In the early church, only those who had seen the Lord after his resurrection could be apostles. Paul was now an apostle himself, and when this was disputed he was able to say, *Am I not an apostle? Have I not seen Jesus our Lord?* (1 Corinthians 9:1).

This appearance to Paul was as real as any other appearance mentioned in his list of witnesses. Peter, the Twelve, the five hundred men, James and the apostles had seen the Lord. Paul then added his own testimony that he, too, had seen and spoken with him on that road to Damascus.

8 The Witnesses Examined

Once witnesses have given their evidence, the next stage in a legal case is to examine and assess it. The evidence of these witnesses is outstanding.

1. Their accounts of the resurrection are independent of each other. On a superficial reading there may appear to be points of disagreement, but closer examination reveals that they are complementary and not contradictory. This is exactly what a lawyer would expect from independent witnesses. Any court would be suspicious of witnesses who agreed with each other word for word. This would show that they must have got together and agreed on what they were going to say. What is impressive is a number of witnesses unanimously testifying to the same thing, each describing it in their own way. This is what we have here.

2. The number of witnesses involved is impressive. *Phipson on Evidence* states 'As a general rule, courts may act on the testimony of a single witness... and where that testimony is unimpeached they should act on it. One credible witness outweighs any number of other witnesses.' However corroboration, while not essential, is always desirable, as it can turn a probability into a certainty. This is what we have here: not just the account of one person who saw Jesus, but twelve separate accounts involving over five hundred people. The evidence of one backs up the evidence of the others.

Furthermore, some of these witnesses saw Jesus on more occasions than one; Peter saw him six times, John, James and Nathanael five times, and Thomas and the other apostles four times.

3. These witnesses either wrote as eyewitnesses of the resurrection or recorded eyewitness accounts of it. On the whole, their evidence was first-hand and not hearsay. Hearsay evidence is what David told Rachel who told Stephen who told me! Normally, such evidence is not allowed by a judge as it is open to abuse, and a story can all too easily change in the telling. As Professor F. F. Bruce has pointed out, 'The earliest preachers of the gospel knew the value of first hand testimony and appealed to it time and time again. "We are witnesses of these things" was their constant and confident assertion. And it can have been by no means so easy as some writers seem to think to invent words and deeds of Jesus in those early years, when so many of his disciples were about, who could remember what had and had not happened.'

4. This evidence is empirical; it is based on observation and experience and not on theory. It is the very kind of evidence which this modern age demands. That which can be seen with the human eye, heard by the human ear and touched by the human hand. This is what we have in the Gospel accounts. These early disciples tell us that they saw Christ for themselves, and, as already mentioned, on one occasion more than five hundred people saw him at once. They also heard Christ speak to them and, in fact, the two walking to Emmaus talked with him for more than two hours. We also find that Mary Magdalene and the others *held him by the feet* (Matthew 28:9). They touched Jesus. The three highest senses we have, sight, hearing and touch, were all involved.

5. In a court of law the character of a witness is always important. *Phipson on Evidence* states 'The credibility of a witness depends upon his knowledge of the facts, his intelligence, his

disinterestedness, his integrity, his veracity. Proportioned to these is the degree of credit his testimony deserves from the court or jury.'

The witnesses for the resurrection include men and women of outstanding character, whose evidence would be accepted in any court of law. Sometimes it is said that these witnesses were simple men and women who would believe anything, or that Jesus appeared only to his disciples. This is simply not the case.

One of the greatest witnesses for the resurrection is the Apostle Paul. No one can possibly say that he was simple. After all, he was a lawyer! As such, he had a mind able to sift evidence and even a cursory reading of his letters will show that he was a man of great intellect. Nor can it be said that Paul was one of the early disciples. His whole background as a Pharisee was against the Christian faith. He was Public Enemy No. 1 of the early church. Yet on his way to Damascus to persecute the Christians there, he met the risen Jesus. From that moment onwards his whole life was changed.

Paul's conversion was no half-hearted affair. It was thorough and enduring. Not only did he stop persecuting the early Christians, but he probably became the greatest Christian who has ever lived. He was hated, persecuted, stoned, flogged, imprisoned, shipwrecked and finally suffered death — all for his faith in the living Jesus. Though in his list of witnesses for the resurrection Paul puts himself last, in many ways he should be first, because he is probably the greatest witness of all to the truth of the resurrection.

9 Circumstantial Evidence

The witness of the disciples is extremely strong direct evidence for Christ's resurrection, and it would be accepted in any court of law. Besides this direct evidence we also have what lawyers call 'circumstantial evidence.' As we have seen, direct evidence deals with the fact in issue, namely, 'Did Christ rise from the dead?' Circumstantial evidence is different. It deals with other facts from which the fact in issue may be inferred. For example, in a murder case the evidence of a witness who saw the accused shoot the dead man is direct evidence. But evidence that the accused purchased a gun, that his fingerprints were found on it and that the bullet which caused death was fired from the same gun is circumstantial evidence. In a court of law, circumstantial evidence can be as valuable as direct evidence. In fact, sometimes it is even better, as direct evidence can be more easily fabricated than a strong chain of circumstantial evidence. If the direct evidence for the miracle of Christ's resurrection is strong, then the circumstantial evidence makes it even stronger. There are four things which cannot be explained unless the miracle of the resurrection took place.

The life of Jesus

It must be admitted straightaway that it is extremely difficult to believe that an ordinary person could die and then rise again from the dead. But Jesus Christ was certainly no ordinary person. Whilst many today are hostile to the church, we still find that they are friendly to Jesus Christ. This is demonstrated by the fact that some 18 million viewed the two episodes of *Jesus of Nazareth* on British television. At one time there was an advertisement in national newspapers about Jesus: 'Born in poverty. Lived only 33 years. Spent most of his life in obscurity. Never wrote a book. Never had any position in public life. Was crucified with two thieves. And yet 2,000 years later, more than 950 million people follow him.'

Jesus Christ is certainly unique. No one has ever taught as he taught. No one has ever lived as he lived. No one has ever made the claims which he made for himself. Even unbelievers have admitted this and paid tribute to the teaching and character of Jesus. Atheist and philosopher Bertrand Russell said, 'There are a good many points upon which I agree with Christ a great deal more than the professing Christians do!'

Albert Einstein once said in an interview, 'No man can deny the fact that Jesus existed, nor that his sayings are beautiful. No man can read the Gospels without feeling the actual presence of Jesus. His personality pulsates in every word. I am a Jew but am enthralled by the luminous figure of the Nazarene.'

No one can accuse any of these people of being Christians. Yet, in a court of law, favourable evidence like this by witnesses from the opposing side would carry great weight. By common consent Jesus is considered to be the greatest man who has ever lived. This being so, it is not so difficult to believe another unique thing about him; namely, that he rose from the dead. As Henry Drummond said some years ago: 'Maybe it is as normal for a sinless man to rise from the dead, as it is for a sinful man to remain in the grave.' The teaching and life of Jesus offer overwhelming circumstantial evidence for the miracle of his resurrection.

The change in the disciples

Jesus' crucifixion was shattering to his disciples. It left them stunned, leaderless and in complete despair. All their hopes were ended. But then something happened. Suddenly these same disciples were utterly changed and became completely different.

Certainly the story of how Peter denied three times that he knew Jesus must be genuine. No one would write such a story about the leader of a movement unless it actually happened. Yet some 50 days later on the day of Pentecost this same Peter risked his life by boldly telling the whole of Jerusalem that he had seen Jesus alive from the dead.

Shortly afterwards, Peter was imprisoned because of his bold witness for Christ, and eventually died for his faith. What changed Peter from the coward that he was to the great disciple that he became? Peter's answer is that he met the risen Christ. Nothing short of this will do.

Thomas had the same experience. He is the most modern-minded of all the disciples, always questioning and looking for proof. When the other disciples said that they had seen Jesus alive, Thomas was incredulous and unbelieving. 'Unless I see I will not believe' was his reaction. One week later Thomas saw Jesus and cried out, 'My Lord and my God.' Thomas the doubter became Thomas the Apostle, and probably the first missionary to India. The change in his life was certainly not wish-fulfilment. Thomas never expected to see the risen Christ, and yet he did.

James, the brother of Jesus, is another whose life was completely changed. Prior to the resurrection he and his brothers did not believe in Jesus. But when we read the history of the early church we find that James, after Peter was imprisoned, rose to prominence as head of the church in Jerusalem. The change in his attitude was so great that he eventually described himself as *a slave of Jesus Christ* (James 1:1).

Peter, Thomas and James are just three among many who had the same experience. Something tremendous must have happened to transform their lives in this way. Without the resurrection of Jesus we have no other explanation for this change. The existence of Christianity is a historical fact which demands an explanation. Any such explanation must acknowledge four basic facts about the early church.

Its origin

Humanly speaking, the early disciples faced an impossible task. Within seven weeks of the death of Jesus, they began their mission to the very city that crucified him. Jerusalem knew the facts about Christ; it could not be hoodwinked. It was the most difficult place of all. Yet it was here that the disciples boldly proclaimed, "*This Jesus God raised up, and of that we all are witnesses*" (Acts 2:32).

Immediately upon hearing about Jesus being alive, over three thousand became Christians. Shortly after, a further five thousand men believed, as well as a large number of the priests. Something phenomenal must have happened for such an impact to be made. Without the resurrection, Christianity would never have got off the ground. The odds against it were too great.

Its members

We hear much today about conflict between those of different races. This is nothing new. At the time of Christ there was conflict between the Roman Gentiles and the Jews whose country had been occupied by them. Yet we find that the members of the early church were both Jews and Gentiles. The conflict between them had been resolved. They were now one in their experience of the power of the living Christ. Within fifteen years of the resurrection Paul could write to the churches of Galatia, *There is neither Jew nor Greek... for you are all one in Christ Jesus* (Galatians 3:28). How could this come about without the miracle of the resurrection? As Daniel Fuller has pointed out, 'To try to explain this without reference to the resurrection is as hopeless as trying to explain Roman history without reference to Julius Caesar.'

Its worship

The Jews kept the Sabbath day, Saturday, as their day of worship, but from an early date the Christians kept the Sunday. This change was remarkable, especially as the early church was made up mainly of converted Jews, who were fanatical observers of the Sabbath. What, then, lay behind this sudden change? The answer is found in an early second-century document known as the *Epistle of Barnabas*: 'Therefore we keep the eighth day with joyfulness, the day on which Jesus rose from the dead.' Only the resurrection can explain the keeping of Sunday as a day of worship.

Its growth

If the resurrection was not true, the early church would have lost its initial momentum and fizzled out. But this is not the case. Despite tremendous persecution the early church multiplied. Remarkable confirmation of this comes from the catacombs in Rome. The Romans cremated their dead, but the early Christians believed in the resurrection of the body and buried their dead in underground cemeteries or catacombs.

Around Rome stretch 600 miles of catacombs where during the first three centuries of Christianity nearly four million Christians were buried. It has been calculated that at one stage at least one-fifth of Rome's population were Christians, and that throughout the Roman Empire in the first three centuries AD 20 million became Christians. Each of these is a witness to the faith of the early church in the resurrection.

The dramatic growth of the early church continued. In Deansgate, Manchester, a word-square was discovered on a piece of pottery in a late second century rubbish pit. It is generally thought that the words on it have a Christian significance, which would make it the first evidence we have for Christianity in Britain. Similar word-squares have been found in Pompeii and Budapest. This shows how quickly the Christian faith spread within a short time to what was then a remote corner of the Roman Empire. To sum up, Christianity is one of the greatest movements in the world's history. It can only be accounted for by an initial impact of colossal drive and power. The existence of Christianity requires the miracle of the resurrection of Christ.

The experience of Christians

From the first Easter Sunday until today there is an unbroken succession of millions who can witness that their lives have been revolutionised by contact with the living Christ. Rich and poor, educated and uneducated, people of different backgrounds, nationalities, cultures and temperaments unite in uniform testimony to the truth of the resurrection. Amongst them are four modern witnesses, all from different denominations of the Christian Church but testifying to the same experience.

The first is that remarkable woman, Commissioner Catherine Bramwell-Booth, the granddaughter of General Booth, founder of the Salvation Army, who died in 1987 aged 104. No one can say that conversions do not last! For 100 years she knew the presence of the living Jesus with her day by day. Her testimony is:

> I was four years old or thereabouts when I gave myself to Christ. I had been naughty. I had grieved my mother. I don't know now what it was... My mother was praying with me, and she prayed with me that the Lord Jesus would forgive me. I don't remember exactly what she said; I wish I could. Then she said to me, 'Now, Cath, you pray, darling; tell Jesus you want to be good.' Well I prayed and did as she said — I promised... I prayed and gave myself to Christ. That, I think, was my first step.

There could hardly be any greater contrast between the simple worship of the Salvation Army and the ceremonial of the Russian Orthodox Church. Its leader in Britain until his death in 2003 was

Archbishop Anthony Bloom. He had, as a young man, a similar experience. He picked up Mark's Gospel and started to read about Jesus. This is what happened:

> Before I reached the third chapter, I suddenly became aware that on the other side of my desk there was a presence. And the certainty was so strong that it was Christ standing there that it has never left me. This was the real turning-point. Because Christ was alive and I had been in his presence I could say with certainty that what the Gospel said about the crucifixion of the prophet of Galilee was true, and the centurion was right when he said, 'Truly he is the Son of God.'

Yet another witness was the broadcaster and writer Malcolm Muggeridge. He tells how, when he was making a film for the BBC in the Holy Land, he too experienced the presence of Christ. This happened while he was walking with a friend along that road to Emmaus where Jesus met those two disciples:

> As my friend and I walked along like Cleopas and his friend, we recalled as they did the events of the crucifixion and its aftermath in the light of our utterly different and yet similar world. Nor was it a fancy that we too were joined by a third presence. And I tell you that wherever the walk, and whoever the wayfarers, there is always this third presence ready to emerge from the shadows and fall in step along the dusty, stony way.

Evidence like this, which could be multiplied a million times, cannot be ignored; it is contemporary and personal testimony to the power of the living Christ. Real Christianity is not ancient history but current events. Jesus is still alive today, changing people's lives, and the experience of Christians all down the ages confirms this.

10 So What?

There is a story about a minister who was given the opportunity of visiting a local factory and speaking to the men in their lunch break. The idea was that if they would not go to church then the church would come to them. But as he introduced his talk on 'Einstein's theory of relativity in relation to the Christian concept of God', it became quickly obvious that his message was completely irrelevant to his captive congregation!

That may be an extreme example, but it does illustrate the way that some people might think of the evidence for the resurrection. 'So what? Even if Jesus did rise from the dead, what does it mean to me?' Let me spell out the implications if the resurrection is true:

It shows that Jesus is God

Everyone must have asked the basic question at one time or another, 'Is there a God?' In other words, is the universe just a closed system or is there an eternal being behind it all? Certainly there is no question more far-reaching in its implications than this. The Jewish philosopher, Mortimer Adler, has said 'The whole tenor of human life is affected by whether men regard themselves as supreme beings in the universe or acknowledge a super-human being whom they conceive of as an object of fear or love, a force to be defied or a lord to be obeyed.'

When I became a Christian, I realised that the resurrection is the greatest proof that there is a God who came into this world in the person of Jesus Christ. Jesus made many remarkable claims about himself. He claimed to be eternal: *"Before Abraham was born, I am!"* (John 8:58). Others are born to live but Jesus said he lived before he was born! He claimed that he was sinless (John 8:46) and that he had the right to forgive sins (Mark 2:10). But the greatest of his claims was that he was God. He said, *"Whoever has seen me has seen the Father"* (John 14:9) and *"I and the Father are one"* (John 10:30).

When challenged to give a sign to show that these claims were true, he refused. Instead, he made the credibility of these claims depend on his resurrection. *"An evil and adulterous generation seeks for a sign, but no sign will be given to it except the sign of the prophet Jonah. For just as Jonah was three days and three nights in the belly of the great fish, so will the Son of Man be three days and three nights in the heart of the earth"* (Matthew 12:39).

The resurrection is the great proof that these claims are true. It validates them. Jesus is eternal, sinless and none other than God himself. As Paul says, *he was declared to be the Son of God in power according to the Spirit of holiness by his resurrection from the dead* (Romans 1:4). To put it more simply, God has landed in this world in the form of Jesus, and the great proof of all this is that he rose again from the dead on the third day.

It means that Jesus is Judge

Jesus not only claimed to be God but also that one day he will judge the whole world. Judgment is not a popular subject. No one relishes going to court and facing man's judgment. Likewise, no one likes the idea of God's judgment.

C. S. Lewis summed up well today's attitude toward God and judgment: 'The ancient man approached God (or even the gods) as the accused person approaches his judge. For the modern man the roles are reversed. He is the judge: God is in the dock. He is quite a kindly judge; if God should have a reasonable defence for being the God who permits war, poverty and disease, he is ready to listen to it. The trial may even end in God's acquittal. But the important thing is that Man is on the Bench and God in the Dock.'

But the Bible says the opposite. It warns us that Jesus is the Judge and that one day we will be in the dock. How do we know that? Again, the resurrection is the answer.

When Paul was on Mars Hill in Athens he saw an altar erected 'To the Unknown God.' This distressed him so much that he preached the good news about Jesus and the resurrection. He not only rebuked the men of Athens for their idolatry but he also spoke about the true and living God: *he commands all people everywhere to repent, because he has fixed a day on which he will judge the world in righteousness by a man whom he has appointed; and of this he has given assurance to all by raising him from the dead"* (Acts 17:30, 31). Paul makes the resurrection of Jesus the proof of the coming day of judgment.

When Jesus was on earth he declared that the Father had entrusted all judgment to him. He further claimed, *"an hour is coming, and is now here, when the dead will hear the voice of the Son of God, and those who hear will live. For as the Father has life in himself, so he has granted the Son also to have life in himself. And he has given him authority to execute judgment, because he is the Son of Man"* (John 5:25-27). People rejected this claim and so hated Jesus that they plotted to have him killed. Nevertheless, Jesus repeated this claim at his trial. When cross-examined by Caiaphas, the high priest, and asked whether he was the Son of God, he replied, *"You have said so. But I tell you, from now on you will see the Son of Man seated at the right hand of Power and coming on the clouds of heaven."* Then the high priest tore his robes and said, *"He has uttered blasphemy. What further witnesses do we need? You have now heard his blasphemy. What is your judgment?"* They answered, *"He deserves death"* (Matthew 26:64-66).

The court record is clear. Jesus was crucified because of his claim to be the Son of God who would one day judge the world. Men rejected him, but God set his seal to this claim by raising Jesus from the dead. The resurrection points to an absolutely certain judgment day. Jesus will be on the bench and every one of us will be in the dock giving an account of what we have done.

It means forgiveness is available

One of India's great Christian leaders, Bakht Singh, was once asked what aspect of the gospel he stressed when preaching to those of other faiths. Did he preach the love of God? 'No. The human mind is so polluted that if you talk about love it immediately thinks of sex.' Did he talk about the wrath of God? 'No. Indians believe that all the gods are angry. An extra one makes no difference.' He was then asked what his main message was. 'To preach the forgiveness of sins. That is what all of us deep down inside are longing for.'

Bakht Singh was right. This is true not only in India but also in the West. The head of a large mental health hospital once said that he would be able to send half of his patients home cured if only they could be assured of forgiveness of their sins.

We hear too little nowadays about sin, but it is still there. It is not, as a teenager once said, 'something that parsons have invented to give themselves a job!' What do Christians mean when they talk about sin? The teaching of the Bible is very simple. Sin is wrongdoing. We can do wrong to ourselves, to others and, above all, to God.

There are two things that I have found true of everyone I have ever met. Firstly, each of us has a standard of right and wrong. Some have higher standards than others but the standard is still there. Secondly, if we are honest with ourselves, each of us has fallen short of our own standards.

If we fall short of our own standards, then what about God's standards? Jesus said that the greatest commandment is *"You shall love the Lord your God with all your heart and with all your soul and with all your mind. This is the great and first commandment. And a second is like it: You shall love your neighbor as yourself"* (Matthew 22:37-40).

The Apostle Paul writes in Romans 3:23, *All have sinned and fall short of the glory* [or standard] *of God.* In the words of the General Confession of the Church of England, 'We have left undone those things which we ought to have done; and we have done those things which we ought not to have done.' How then can we obtain forgiveness of our sins? The answer is found in both the cross and the resurrection of Jesus. Leighton Ford has pointed out that the cross answers three great questions:

> Is forgiveness necessary? Yes, we answer, look at Jesus on the cross! There most clearly we see the curse of sin. Is forgiveness possible? Yes, we answer, look at Jesus on the cross! His blood shed for us is the pledge of God's love to the sinner. But is forgiveness just? Yes, we answer again, look at Jesus on the cross! God did not make light of sin. Rather, the Judge allowed himself to be judged in our place to transform us by his grace.

The resurrection also answers a fourth great question. Is forgiveness available? Was the death of Jesus sufficient to take away our sins? The answer of the resurrection is 'Yes.' *He was delivered up for our trespasses and raised for our justification* (Romans 4:25).

The resurrection is like a receipt you are given when you pay a debt. The receipt does not pay the debt; it is evidence that the debt has been paid. In the same way, when Jesus died on the cross he paid the debt of sin. The punishment which should have been ours fell on him. The resurrection three days later is God's great receipt and proof to us that the debt of sin has been paid. Forgiveness is available.

It gives meaning to life

On one occasion, the senior partner of a leading London firm of solicitors wrote an article in a law magazine in which he quoted with approval the advice, 'Every lawyer in private practice ought to spend at least one hour per day sitting with his feet on the desk, his hands behind his head, gazing into space thinking where he is, where he wants to go and how he is going to get there.' He then wrote about strategic planning in running a law practice. Lawyers need to plan for the future and think about where their firm is going. I wrote to him agreeing with what he had to say, but saying also that it is short sighted to plan one's career carefully without thinking about the real meaning of life. One basic question every one of us needs to face up to is, what is the meaning of life? Why are we here? What is it all about?

This came home to me vividly some years ago when I was one of the managers of a special school for boys who had committed crimes. In trying to decide whether the boys I was responsible for could leave and go home, I asked each one if they knew why they were at the school. I particularly wanted to see if they understood they were there to be helped rather than to be punished. To my surprise and sadness, I found that not one of about a dozen boys I questioned had any clear idea of why they were really there. It would seem to be the first question they would have asked. But they were typical of so many of us today, rushing through life without ever stopping to ask what the purpose of it all is.

The Apostle Paul wrote: *For to me to live is Christ.* Each of us came into this world not to live just for ourselves but to fulfil the purpose that Christ has for our lives. If Jesus rose from the dead, then he is with us day by day. He gives us a reason for living and makes the whole of life worthwhile. As he said, "*I came that they may have life and have it abundantly*" (John 10:10).

It gives hope in the face of death

Over 3,000 years ago Job asked *"If a man dies, shall he live again?"* (Job 14:14). Ever since then, philosophers and thinkers have tried to answer his question, but in vain. Nowadays death is the last thing we want to talk about. In a nervous way we make jokes about it. Like the American comedian Woody Allen who quipped, 'I'm not afraid of death; I just don't want to be there when it happens!'

The writer C. S. Lewis came face to face with death many times. First, when he was nine and lost his grandfather, uncle and mother all in the same year. Later, as a young man during the First World War, he lost many of his army friends. Finally, the woman he married late in life died of cancer. He summed up today's attitude toward death with these words: 'There are, aren't there, only three things we can do about death: to desire it; to fear it; or to ignore it.' The latter attitude is certainly the most common.

But there are certain things about death which everyone must agree with. First, it is certain. As George Bernard Shaw said 'The statistics about death are very impressive. One out of one dies!' Despite this, we have a strange attitude toward it. When it happens to someone else we regard it as quite ordinary. Somehow we never think of it happening to us, but of course it will.

Also, death is unpredictable. I constantly had to deal with the estates of clients of my firm who had died unexpectedly. Although death is certain, no one knows the day or the hour when it is coming. As the Danish proverb puts it, 'Death does not blow a trumpet.'

Above all death is the ultimate. It is so final. Everything that people hold dear — whether genius, love, wealth or power — is utterly bankrupt in its presence. The old Puritan was right when he said 'At death all the pieces on the chessboard of life, the King, the Queen, the Rook, the Bishop, the Knight and the Pawn are swept into the same box.' Anyone who has not seriously thought about death has never really faced the ultimate — indeed we often seem to think that we are immortal.

Is there an answer to Job's age-old question, 'Is there life after death?' Shakespeare in *Hamlet* describes death as 'The undiscover'd country from whose bourn no traveller returns.' But he is wrong. If Jesus rose from the dead, then someone has returned. He has come back from death itself.

C. S. Lewis, in his book *Miracles*, writes: 'Jesus has forced open a door that has been locked since the death of the first man. He has met, fought, and beaten the King of Death. Everything is different because he has done so. This is the beginning of the New Creation. A new chapter in cosmic history has opened.'

Death is not the end. Jesus rose from the dead. There is hope.

11 Your Verdict

To use a legal term, the case for the resurrection rests. In a court case this means that the legal argument has ended and it is time to give a verdict.

You will recall that a member of a jury has two duties. The first one is to be unbiased. This is not as easy as it seems. I like the story about the man who thought he was dead. His wife and friends were so worried that they sent him to a psychiatrist, who determined to cure him by convincing him of one fact that contradicted his belief that he was dead. He decided to use the simple truth that dead men do not bleed. So he put his patient to work reading medical books. After some weeks the patient finally said, 'Alright, alright! You have convinced me. Dead men do not bleed.' The psychiatrist then stuck a needle in his arm and the blood flowed out. The man looked down with a contorted, ashen face and cried out, 'Good Lord! Dead men bleed after all!'

This story is not so far removed from real life. Professor Sir Norman Anderson tells how he once gave a talk at a university on the resurrection. He presented the evidence and showed how all the rival explanations were unsatisfactory. A professor of philosophy in the audience agreed that the other explanations were inadequate, but insisted that, despite this, the resurrection simply could not have happened. Sir Norman replied, 'May I paraphrase what you have just said? If you do not want to believe in the resurrection, you won't.' The unbelief of the professor was not because of the evidence; it was in spite of it. When challenged about this, the professor admitted this was true. His bias was obvious.

The second duty of a jury is to give a verdict. The staggering implications of the resurrection demand this. Christ's return from the dead is either the greatest thing that ever happened or the biggest deception of all times. No sane thinking person can be neutral about it. Yet when speaking on this subject I have often found that people are reluctant to come to a conclusion. At one student meeting, when asked to give a verdict on the resurrection, about a quarter of the students abstained! In a debate this is admissible. But in a court of law the members of a jury cannot abstain. The decision they have to make is too important. The same applies to the resurrection. This is no debating point; eternal issues are at stake.

I would like to ask for your verdict on two key questions about the resurrection of Jesus.

Do you believe that Jesus rose from the dead?

Our original question, 'What happened to Jesus?' still demands an answer. We have considered the various explanations that have been given but none of them stands up to close examination. I maintain that the only reasonable one is that the miracle of the resurrection took place. On one occasion a book by an Orthodox Jew on the resurrection of Jesus was featured in the 'Religion' section of *Time*. The book startled the Jewish world because, after studying the evidence, its author, Professor Pinchas Lapide, said: 'I accept the resurrection of Easter Sunday not as an invention of the community of disciples, but as a historical event.'

I have already mentioned how the lawyer, Frank Morison, changed his mind and became convinced of the resurrection of Jesus as he carefully studied the evidence. The same happened to Charles Colson. Lawyers are not generally noted for their Christian faith, but they do know when something is proved.

Lord Caldecote, once Lord Chief Justice of England, has written:

> My faith began with and was founded on what I
> thought was revealed in the Bible. When, particularly, I
> came to the New Testament, the Gospels and other
> writings of the men who had been friends of Jesus
> Christ seemed to me to make an overwhelming case,
> merely as a matter of strict evidence, for the facts
> therein stated... The same approach to the cardinal
> test of the claims of Jesus Christ, namely, his
> resurrection has led me as often as I have tried to
> examine the evidence to believe it as a fact beyond
> dispute.

Another former Lord Chief Justice of England, Lord Darling, once
said:

> We, as Christians, are asked to take a very great deal
> on trust; the teachings, for example, and the miracles
> of Jesus. If we had to take all on trust, I, for one,
> should be sceptical. The crux of the problem of
> whether Jesus was, or was not, what he proclaimed
> himself to be, must surely depend upon the truth or
> otherwise of the resurrection. On that greatest point
> we are not merely asked to have faith. In its favour as a
> living truth there exists such overwhelming evidence,
> positive and negative, factual and circumstantial, that
> no intelligent jury in the world can fail to bring in a
> verdict that the resurrection story is true.

I have proved for myself that this is the case. During the last thirty
years I must have spoken on the evidence for the resurrection at
least three hundred times. In order to involve my audience, at the
end of my talk I sometimes ask for a verdict. By a show of hands

those present have to vote for one of the four options — fraud, swoon, delusion or miracle.

At one student meeting, though nearly all my audience were not Christians, three-quarters of them voted in favour of the miracle of the resurrection. Perhaps this should not have surprised me since the evidence for it is so strong. But it is not sufficient to believe that Jesus rose from the dead. Something more is required of us.

Many times I have been asked why, if the evidence for the resurrection is so strong, everyone does not believe in it. The answer is that becoming a Christian involves not just our intellects, but also our wills. Though the Christian faith stands up to examination and is based on trustworthy evidence, many people reject it for a deeper reason than mere intellectual objection. Very often their rejection is due to an unwillingness to surrender control of their lives to Jesus Christ.

Pride also often stops us from becoming Christians. We fail to realise our need and are reluctant to admit we are wrong. All of us are fond of ourselves. A wit once said, 'The average person is a self-made man who worships his creator!' Above all, the greatest obstacle to faith in Christ is the change that this would require in our lives. The real trouble is not that we cannot believe but that we will not believe — despite the evidence. I have a simple test for finding out the sincerity of those who raise objections to the resurrection. I ask the question, 'If I were able to prove to you beyond a shadow of a doubt that Jesus was raised from the dead, would you then become a Christian?' Sadly, I find that very often the answer is 'No. It would involve too much of a change in my life.' The real difficulty is not intellectual but moral.

Do you know Jesus Christ as a living person?

Professor Robert Boyd, in his booklet *Can God Be Known?*, pointed out that there are three kinds of knowledge. First, there is mathematical or logical knowledge. An example of this from school days is the theorem of Pythagoras. Secondly, there is scientific knowledge — hypothesis followed by an experiment. It is this type of knowledge which has enabled man to travel to the moon. Thirdly, there is personal knowledge. This is the kind of knowledge we refer to when we say, 'Oh yes, I know her well.' This knowledge involves an encounter with someone else. It is based on a relationship.

It is personal knowledge that is involved in becoming a Christian. It is all too easy to give a mental assent to the truths of Christianity without an encounter with the living Jesus. Logic is not enough. If Jesus rose from the dead, then he is alive today. This is what it means to be a Christian: to know Christ as our living Saviour, who has forgiven our sins and changed our lives.

As you finish reading I would like you to consider your verdict. This is the most important thing on which you will ever be asked to make a decision. It demands careful consideration by every one of us. Lawyers may present the evidence, but every legal case ends with the judge turning to the members of the jury and saying, 'Ladies and gentlemen of the jury, the verdict is yours.'

It's your turn now. What is your verdict about Jesus? Did he rise from the dead? And if he did, what are the implications for you, and for your own life and death?

12 A Step Further

If you have been convinced that Christ rose from the dead, but have never come to know him as a living Saviour, I would like to explain exactly what it means to become a Christian. If you are not ready to take this step, can I recommend instead that you carefully read at least one of the Gospel accounts of the life, death and resurrection of Jesus. It would be tragic for you to miss the truth by failing to study the evidence in more detail for yourself.

In taking the step of personally accepting the claims of Christ on your life, there are two things that you need to know and one thing that you must do. Firstly, you need to know your own need in the sight of God. If we are honest with ourselves, every one of us has sinned against God. We have fallen short not only of our own standards but also of God's standards. We have left God out of our lives.

Secondly, not only do you need to know the bad news about yourself, but also the good news about Jesus. The very heart of the gospel is *that Christ died for our sins in accordance with the Scriptures, that he was buried, that he was raised on the third day in accordance with the Scriptures...* (1 Corinthians 15:3, 4).

Lastly, there is one thing you must do. It is not enough to know that we are sinners and that Jesus died for us and is alive today. God's forgiveness must be accepted.

Some years ago in America there was an unusual legal case which illustrates this. A man called George Wilson was indicted for robbing a mail van and nearly killing its driver. He was condemned to death for this but shortly before his execution he was pardoned by the President. Amazingly, when he heard of this, he refused to accept the pardon and said that he wanted to die. This raised the question as to whether a pardon had to be accepted to be valid. Despite his protests, George Wilson's lawyer obtained a stay of execution. He contended that his client could not be executed because he had been pardoned. The case was brought to the Supreme Court of the United States and its decision read as follows:

> A pardon is a deed, to the validity of which delivery is essential; and delivery is not complete without acceptance. It may be then rejected... and if it be rejected, we have discovered no power in a court to force it on him. It may be supposed that no one being condemned to death would reject a pardon, but the rule must be the same.

The sad result was that because George Wilson would not accept his pardon he was executed and died by his own choice.

In the same way the pardon which God offers us must be accepted to be of any value to us. We need to pray to the living Jesus, asking him to forgive our sins and to change our lives. When I did this at the age of eighteen my whole life was dramatically changed. Jesus Christ is willing to do the same for you.

Our part is to ask Jesus, through prayer, to make this great change in our lives. And if you find prayer difficult, may I suggest that you use a simple prayer like this: Lord Jesus Christ, I confess that I have sinned against you. I thank you for dying on the cross for me and that you are alive today. I come to you just as I am. I want to know you in a real way. Forgive my sin. Change my life. Show yourself to me and be my Saviour and Lord. Amen.

Don't think that prayer alone makes you a Christian! You will need to find a church where the Bible is believed and taught. You (and others!) will see a real change in your life as you turn from sin to those things that please God.

In conclusion, let me offer some practical advice to those who have sincerely prayed this prayer and decided to follow Christ.

1. Tell someone today about your decision.

2. Believe Christ's promise when he says, "*whoever comes to me I will never cast out*" (John 6:37). Rely on his promise, not on your feelings.

3. Find time each day to pray and read a portion from the Bible.

4. Join a Christian church. You need the help that comes from regular worship and fellowship.

5. Begin to pray for your friends and try to win them for Christ. They too need to give a verdict.